CLOSE YOUR EYES
&
READ THIS BOOK

poems by

Nicholas Leon LaFond

BOOK DESIGN AND COVER ART BY KIT ANDERSON
KitAnderson.com // @iKitAnderson

Printed in the United States of America.

CLOSE YOUR EYES
&
READ THIS BOOK

poems by

Nicholas Leon LaFond

FOREWORD

Hello everybody, my name is Nicholas Leon LaFond. This collection of poems, lyrics, musings and observations is compiled from several different notebooks, scraps of paper, receipts, napkins and pocket size notepads. It spans several years of writing that took place in a variety of towns, cities, settings, buildings, vehicles and states of mind. It is a selection of work that I feel is some of my best and/or favorite and that I could still find when I was compiling this book. Some of the more political pieces were written during different and unique social and political landscapes and may be more specific to those eras and less generally reflecting of current or timeless social or political situations. Bear with me.

I thank you for purchasing, borrowing, finding, stealing or at least reading this collection

1.

BREAK THE BLOCK

To start, put pen to paper,

Hand upon instrument.

Move as you are moved

And if nothing stirs you at the moment,

Put your foot forward and step,

And step again and again

Until you have moved yourself,

Then,

Look around you.

AS YOU ARE

Embrace your mediocrity

For it is only through your eyes

You are perceiving.

Encourage those

By whose talents you are impressed

And do not fear them.

Abandon yourself not

For insecurities

Only to make faulty attempts

At the ways of someone else,

As you are yourself

Be also inspired.

3.

EXPLOSIONS IN THE CANOPY

Diaspora of the light green leaves,

The nubile, succulent and tender,

Going the way that each individual leaf

Is blown and flows with the wind.

For the formative times, as nutrients are shared

And the development of sturdy structures

Is to come from a shared source,

Each leaf matures to a deep, verdant tone.

The tone of each leaf varies once again in the next season,

As that which once fed and supported and equally gained

Now retracts that support in effort to save itself,

Leaving the foliage nothing but to be drained its blood,

Strangely leaving each individual brilliant on its own.

In arrays of Vermillion, Fire, Brick, Golden and Brown,

The brief explosion of contrary colouring

Renders each leaf barren of sustenance from the host.

The individuals must fall from the tree

And dry upon the hardening earth,

All the while continuing on a path of destiny

Not, perhaps, even understood

By the former denizens of the canopy.

As they relinquish their loft, they find new purpose

In a new state of being,

As they provide sustenance at root

And bring life to a new generation of Green

Through their decay.

A BRIEF SOJOURN INTO SUMMER

Evening, yet I can still feel

The sun on my face and shoulders,

Reminding me of the brief sojourn into Summer

We received this day.

A creek running,

Laughing over rocks and boulders,

Those walking about

Enjoying such a memory

Come to current, to now,

Becoming a fond experience of discussion,

Laughter and play.

On days like this,

A Winter thaw or birth of Spring,

All seems a dance.

The people, wind and plants,

The natural animals alive with movement

And grace present in all their endeavors.

As if an uncontrived thank you to

Whoever or whatever is responsible

For a day like this.

HEART SHAPED BALLOONS

Old man in oversized suit

Talks to girl on cigarette break.

He makes a balloon,

Offers his heart just to connect

But she talks to distance

And he presses onward.

Balloon laughs in it's lightness

And mocks his heart

With it's shape and it's weight.

In my pity I see his strength

As he moves on.

And looking up,

I find love for the night sky

When it's dark and honest,

The stars piercing but painless.

6.

INDIANA SUNSET

Blazing orange sunset,

It cleanses my eyes of the concrete and billboards.

Those cosmetic distractions,

Commercial cover up

For the natural beauty.

The way the land lays,

Covered in the early evening shadows,

Is graceful and comforting.

These trips across the earthen sea,

These voyages,

Though not without incidents

Of varying welcome,

Are life in the moment

And become the memories which

Tug upwards the corners of the mouth

And pound the heart.

LOOKING BACK ON 7 YEARS

One more dance, a chance

To wreck the stage

And not think about finance.

Bloody heads, chipped teeth and sweat,

Of those times no regrets,

Hours and mileage stakes for gentlemen's bets

On how late, an hour or more,

But still there before the opened door.

Couches and floors,

Atlantic to Pacific shores,

New sisters and brothers,

A family from different mothers.

Tip top shape the band, but not the van,

Swimming in catastrophe

Yet still able to make a stand and

Isn't it grand, traversing the land?

Recognition of the atmosphere,

Talking about the stratosphere,

Asking what you've got,

Knowing more than you've seen here.

Peer to peer becomes much more clear

When you can reach out and touch

That which you hear.

NOT TO FORGET, NOT TO LIVE IN MEMORY

Zip, Boom, Crash!

And that's the last of the excitement

For the night.

The flames that once burned high, consuming,

Now smoldering coals.

But with a breath,

Gust of air and some tinder,

Together with remaining cinder,

And these flames could burn brighter and hotter than

before.

But for reluctant put-off,

Waiting for better

Instead of making due so you can make good,

Doesn't seem progressive, but we shall see

As we move faster towards

What we don't yet know,

I say yet.

Not to forget, but not to live in memory,

Fear is merely a parcel on this voyage

And if the load is too heavy

You can shrug off the superfluous luggage

And travel light,

Seeing we don't need to be sleeping

Even though it's night.

So take off you garments of distress,

Let them fall to the floor!

Be no longer cloaked in doubt and

Dress in it no more.

Power may not seem yours, but

It's no one's over you no how, because

A struggle is no struggle if

No one is holding you down.

So, brave these days

For they are yours to do with and to,

And pay attention to the elders!

They teach with more than their words and attitudes.

Our gift is their past if that's how we see it,

We can learn from their youth, but

We don't have to be it.

For we are young, now, today!

Learning from history!

Notice them now,

Remember what you see, because

Mistakes were made and paths stopped short,

But some ideas were righteous

Despite their abort.

Embrace your young days, yet

Don't fear any age,

For your breath is your work,

Life your wage.

PAINT WITH WORDS

Paint with words, a picture,

A representation

That is up for interpretation

When looked back upon.

"What was I thinking"

Is often asked in different tones

And is usually answered silently.

What pictures we create,

What landscapes,

Retrospect can fuzz the lines,

The borders,

Can make chaos seem like order

Ugliness like something else.

The weather changes,

"Not as much snow as last year,

or rain, neither".

Our life is our own

History belongs to someone else

As we create our past

Realize we have a future.

SUNSHINE AFTER RAIN

(OR, SMILES FROM STRANGERS)

Life is a beautiful thing.

Life… is… beautiful!

No job? No matter, life goes on!

What a vision of beauty,

A sunlit street with lush green topped trees.

Wetted by random rainfall

Only hours ago,

All set against a blue so pure

You just stop for a moment to embrace it,

Breathe the aroma of such a glorious day

And progress,

Feeling that much better for appreciating life,

Allowing the trivial to be trivial.

Far too long been caught up in such insignificant or

Overblown self thought and insecurity,

How can you ignore such natural reality?!

Not just the sunshine either!

Finding enjoyment in getting rained on

During a long walk

To a place that is closed when you get there,

And shrugging off what might be seen as

An inconvenience,

While feeling zen on the walk back to the apartment.

So much is good but overlooked

And understandably so,

Considering where the focus is

In much of our societal influences,

And the importance we learn to place on things

That in turn, cause ours or our neighbor's,

Brother's or sister's,

Unhappiness.

What's more sacred than

A genuine smile from a stranger?

Not one conjured up

Out of politeness or courtesy,

A public curtsy,

But a smile given,

A smile felt!

And their reward,

If one is even necessary,

Is your inspired

Uncontrolled smile in return.

Peace, found in the simplicity

Of the truth of life.

11.

NEIGHBOR STRANGER

What's more sacred than

A smile from a stranger?

Like a brief golden shot

Through clouds, through gray,

And for a minute it seems

Our existence is not in danger,

A chance for hope,

For neighborhoods to perpetuate.

12.

IF I DROPPED A SONG

If I dropped a song in the wilderness,

Would it make a sound?

Would anyone gather around,

For warmth or light?

Would it shine at all

Coming from my head?

From the soul is the reflection

Like the Moon shows the Sun,

Full upon nighttime fields and woods.

If the song does pass

From soul through mind,

If your heart beats truth through every line,

If ideas are seeds

That when sown, show proof in deeds,

Then the hearts of the world

Your song will find.

13.

IT'S ABOUT TIME I WROTE YOU A SONG

You look at me and you ask if I think you're crazy

I say no then I ask you why you're with me

You reply by asking me the same thing

I say that it must be because we're both amazing.

On snow covered streets and shit covered sidewalks

We got to know each other well

While watching where we stepped we always spoke freely

It never hurt very much when we fell.

Looking at the snowflakes and seeing stars

We kept each other warm both night and day

Not much room on my single bed where we'd lay

That was fine we'd spent enough time being far away.

When you decided to move back to your hometown

I didn't recommend it but I said that I understand

Because while on your sunny coast we reconfirmed suspicions

That you and I were more than a flash in the pan.

It's about time I wrote you a song

It's not too short and it's not too long

It just says that I remember

How it is we really got together

And that I think about our love that we share

And if you ever wondered before,

Let this be a sign

To show you that I care,

I love you.

CUBES AND SPHERES

Push me over the edge

So that I may fall into grace.

Stumbling through these days,

My mind is flailing, my heart is wailing.

It's not where you are, it's what you are,

And that comes down to who you are.

Flaccid tongues that wag a lot

Might even be able to hit the spot,

But tell you nothing about what's real.

Intent to steal, they've nothing to feel

But desperate lashing, gold leaf a-flashing,

They fear your opened eyes,

They fear fresh air on their lies.

Gathering flies, they carry on with their carrion

Banking the wool will stay in place.

And now I see, boxes have edges,

No more than obnoxious ledges.

Rigid lines to confine, empty rules for to adhere.

Lovely gardens obscured by hedges

Made to sharp points, laid as wedges

To block eyes of minds, to confound what is clear.

And through this, the grace I sought I've found

By pulling away the wool, and looking around.

The cubes still exist, as I persist

And realize a sphere.

15.

HER FIRST LETTER AFTER OUR FIRST KISS

Unworthy.

Sweet thoughtful words on page

And I unworthy

Of the adjectives and metaphors.

Who knows but one who feels the middle,

Between the casual surface

And the intimate deep,

Where lives caress.

Is it the idea? The anticipation?

The space filled?

These questions

Perhaps too subjective for

Such fresh happenings.

Cautious of affection.

TO SEE BEYOND THE ARCHITECTURE

The dawn is racing to the shore,

But it's hard to see it anymore

When our eyes are covered up

By plastic mouths that lie

About a golden cup.

Thieving hands steal windowpanes

While we don't notice when it rains.

"Hush now child, don't worry about what's real,

We will hide that all away and help you forget

How to feel."

And the skies, they've opened up so wide

To show a reflection of what's died.

Those who say they have touched the sun have lied,

Just ask any of the fallen who have tried.

It's not conspiracy, just business

And in this business, hope is a dangerous mistress.

Not all horses led to shores will drink

But most folks will go anywhere if you tell them,

If you sell them, how to think.

And all the races that are run

For the benefit of someone

Who cares not of your sweat and blood,

Who would throw you face first in the mud,

They mean nothing to your day

If you have the strength to walk away,

And drive your flag into the land

And obliterate any line in the sand.

COTTON STEEL

Pouring, steady soft

Time spent feels as if lost.

Tight rope, apex perch,

Heart pounds as day does lurch.

Gray grove somehow does nourish

Notions of the purest

Amorous and vexing feelings,

Yet, just to live here feels like stealing.

Soft and dull, beautiful and cold

As the cotton steel sky

Rains down upon the roses and the crows.

Trudging through the day

All is new but feels the same

Throughout life apology

For blue skies that are not seen

Longing for a place

Hoping for just a taste

Of memories that made me joyful

But for the future I'm hopeful.

Soft and dull, beautiful and cold

As the cotton steel sky

Rains down upon the roses and the crows

And Spring blooms.

PASSIVE TO THE POINT OF DESPERATION

My heart aches for want of new,

My heart yearns for want of old.

I have no sanctity left,

All my personal places have been destroyed.

My feelings of betrayal

Manifest in my inaction,

Poems come as suicide notes,

Though my intention is not

In killing anyone but my idle self.

Stale sweat of couch sleep

Chokes my thoughts

And I wish there was another continent,

A place where maybe I could run

To happiness.

But I know, even in fantasy

That would be short lived.

A hero!

I sculpted in my mind

A picture of myself as a hero!

Only to awake to an

Ineffectual promiser of alchemy,

Leaden life to golden dreams.

I merely dashed hopes,

Though all construct in their own image

For their own gain.

I feel a need to be alone

And let down no one.

Friends are friends

And that is why I should leave.

But will that solve anything?

Such plans,

I need not be present but as memory.

I can live as me,

And do,

But as inspiration is fading

And tepid is my participation,

What but stories and tears have I?

RORSHACH TEST

There's something in the way the

Ink falls on the paper that

Keeps my eyes moving from

Left to right.

A sense of gray matter

Some human content here

Bringing together the

Black and white.

A taste of something good

Delved from a conscious soul,

Delicious apparitions take flight.

But bitter comments are

Sometimes fodder for a

Meal of words to be served

Next night and served cold.

In a forest of trees

It seems that no one sees

The axes coming closer,

But the limbs bend only in the breeze.

And the wind's picked up!

The blades nearly at the trunks!

For how much longer can a forest be?

Or even trees?

In our society so much variety,

But not much verite'

To our day.

We search for loveliness,

Look for it somewhere else,

Rarely hearing what we say.

Why can't a poet just have a conversation?

Why must we grasp at others for our hope?

Why do we blame the hands of those who tie the knots

While we let them make a noose of our own rope?

PAST THE LEAVES

If a Tree falls in the woods

And you are deaf,

Does not the Tree still fall?

The sound it made would matter less.

Why did the Tree fall?

What man's ax,

What god's thunderous bolt,

What did cause that which was so reticently fortified

To topple?

Blood stains the hands but

What first stained the eyes?

The cries of throats complained in hunger,

The Tree did not yield them fruit.

The Sun beat upon flesh burned,

The Tree gave no shade.

No comfort from it's trunk,

No shelter,

And no justice was found

In those who did hang from its limbs.

Such magnificence lost!

Such royal virtue humbled!

But with the sky unobstructed

The azure free and exposed,

We can now see clearly

What it is

That is not there.

21

4 EYES

I guess the time is here

For me to kick something in your ear

So everybody come gather round near

And if you feel like it you can cheer.

I will say what I got to say

The Mathematicians are gonna' play,

If you dig the vibe, go ahead and sway

And if not my friend, be on your way.

A matter of simple ratios,

1+1 in equal parts,

Dancing shoes or plain clothes

Symmetry of beating hearts,

Gyrations that blow up the charts,

Quick stops and quick starts.

Who showed up after the dance floor was blowed up?

This microphone gets tore up,

Then we pull it together like incline planes and levers

Simple machines, you know what I mean?

Driving over medians, Steve McQueen cool

A la mode, ice cream with James Dean

A teenyboppers dream!

And a copper coffee cup full of what's up?

What's up.

Mathematicians lay down grooves

Designed to make your head move,

Up and down, back and forth,

Straight up!

Like 90 degrees or true North.

So open up your aural canal and your cabesa,

Before too long your body may amaze ya'

As you bump to the groove

And move with the rhythm,

Feeling Pete on the bass

And the drums as Al hits them,

Dewey on the keys as you bend at the knees

And say, "Mathematicians? Oh please"

Then, "Oh geez! Gimme more and more

Of those honey sweet beats with the melody on top!"

Mathematicians on the scene the party don't stop,

We kick out the jams, pie charts and diagrams,

No need to cheat on the final exam,

We don't scam.

So pluck a number from the tree,

A squared plus BB and Double C

That's me, Pythagoras

The G plus P to the E, T, E.

When we play a show there's no factions,

No division, no one is a fraction!

We pay attention and vibe on your reactions

And the gloomy moods meet with subtraction.

In perfect attendance or if you skip classes

Don't forget to bring your hall passes

That say, "I'm one of many unique among the masses"

Because life is a series of quizzes and card flashes.

So who cares if your suit clashes?

We're no dance floor fascists!

It's 4 then 4 on the XY axis

So free your mind and wipe your eyeglasses.

22

BENEATH OUR BLANKET

Next to, sideways, no one there.

Memory pictures, pluck them from the air

Because they are all that's left,

To you and me.

The clock it hides but the sun comes up.

I've got to go and you are leaving

Too soon for me,

And it's a shame I only know you

To miss you.

I finish my cold cup of tea

And that is the last

You will see of me

At all, at all, I know,

I know.

Some things aren't meant to be

For more than a little while, I guess.

Love seems like a tangent to me,

Moments where I digress.

When all is said and done,

It's done.

And the rising sun

Does melt the morning fog,

And the fragile amnion

Of the heat beneath our blanket.

I watch you as I leave,

You say to me,

"Just think of me sometimes,"

Sometimes.

And I do, and I do,

Sometimes.

That night was worth an hour of sleep

Before heading down the Northway

To the City

And back the same night in the rain.

And if I thought of it before

I could have met you at the bus stop

For 5 minutes, or an hour more

Before you went

Home.

23

EVERGREEN

I beat upon my bones, my head

You beat upon my confidence, a drum

Twist the knobs till I'm perfectly

Out of tune, though looking for perfect pitch.

Do you like what you see?

And of what you hear?

Be not so superficial,

Ask not what your community can do for you

But what you haven't done for your community.

Desperation gives way to hope,

To desperation, to hope

And it doesn't matter.

Know you are trash, but useful

In a slave-wage sense…

That's not fair! To perceive the kindness of strangers as

poison!

An awkward way with great intentions,

So far, always making an effort for good.

Stay Green, though you may be jaded

In this chamber of blue.

IS IT REALLY ABOUT THE GRIND?

Work to live,

You work until you die.

Where is my life?

Is it at the end of an 8 hour work day?

Is it behind a desk wrapped in shirt and tie?

MOTHER OF THE GARDEN,

LADY OF THE PARKING LOT

She's having fun.

No one really talks to her,

So she talks to everyone.

Says that she's got 13 babies,

Maybe Jesus and the Apostles

Her 13 sons,

And she named everyone.

She tends the garden

That is taken for granted

In its use.

Of all that she has planted,

And is *still* taken for granted,

Her wage for her works,

Casual abuse.

She yells to be heard

And so do the ears close.

No regard for her wild plea

Or the world that she knows,

Her wailing ignored in every word.

Seen only as another noisy bird,

Flightless wings still beating and free

As her desperation grows.

The saints rarely adorned in papal stance

As their acts receive no celebration.

To the eyes, their worth obscured

By hands stained with greed

As they aspire not to adulation.

They hope for tomorrow, and hope upon chance,

That others notice their deeds

And dirty their own hands,

Not from the taking of fruit

But from the pulling of the weeds.

26.

OH, DEER

How dear a deer,

Standing alone in the clear,

All by itself,

Still a deer.

When among the growing herd,

Deer,

Still a deer,

The name for one,

The name for all

Solo or with peer.

How great a name

Which sounds the same

For one or many

Or all.

27

FRUIT FROM THE VINE

When a grape falls from the vine,

For sure it is ready.

But its juice may be not sweet

If only wind, or rot, or beast have made the decision.

The vine holds the fruit

Only long enough

For it to find its way

Toward the beginning of its fate.

The juice, the wine,

The fruit, all defined.

As the time is tolled

And the grape has rolled,

In all intent,

However it all went,

The fruit that fell

Or was picked,

Will become the wine of celebration

Or feed the next.

28

WINTER BIRDS

A call to all

Whose passive life keeps them saying,

"I wish I… I wish I was…",

Feel, sweater off,

Autumn's kiss on bare flesh

One last time,

As the sky hints to Winter

Leaves fall golden down.

I know of no clock to

Tick away death in seconds or days.

There is the guarantee of rest

And time is of value and use.

The heart beats to proclaim

This is the time for life!

What fleeting life

Our existence.

The scope of time so vast

But we are just an instant,

And the tax of death on the gift of our life

Seems fair at times,

When we get a glimpse of life's purpose.

Hear the song of the birds who stay

To challenge the season, Winter's grey,

And the notes are grace flowing from the trees

To reach my ears, hover above brown leaves.

A ringing verse, a singing verse,

A call to all, a call to all,

Resound! Ring forth!

A declaration of life!

Lungs pulling wind,

Pushing song.

29

TO THOSE WHO TEACH

Baby fields of growing minds.

We could be called agriculture.

Seeds planted, ideas harbored,

Thoughts cultivated, if nothing else

Our brain could be produce.

Not to say vegetable, but a growing and effected entity.

Some harvest minds

And turn them into frozen foods

Or worse,

Canned soups.

But some tend to these beautiful specimens

And trim, prune and feed them,

Only in want of being able

To appreciate the fruits produced by them.

Nothing more, nothing less,

Other than a recognition

Of the nursery and horticulturalist

Who did help them grow.

Composting with history and experiences!

Not fertilizing with shop made and

Synthetic rhetoric,

Reflecting a lack of respect for the farm,

Not to mention the crops.

Some who care

Save the plantation

From drought or rocky soil,

Yielding a fine crop

In the face of ever mounting adversity and obstacles.

And I say to the rare few who take pride in their

Agrarian efforts,

You are champions of the field.

30

THE SHEEP REVOLT AGAINST THE SHEPHERD

I can be a mushroom, I can be a panther

I can be a mountain lion, I can be a dancer

In the dark, till a spark lights up brightly

To ignite me, incite me to try it or riot

And I don't buy it when they say to me

That's why they pay me,

To keep quiet and not bother

The dis-figure father

At the top of the trash heap,

Who pacifies to keep sheep

Bleating at his sick teat,

And sings dull-abyes

To close their eyes.

Telling them to disown their black,

But he's scared of words on uprising.

That's not at all surprising,

With people asking, realizing,

What if the heard becomes a pack?

31

FASHION AND VOGUE

The most ridiculous hat is

En vogue for as long as

We don't look back

To then, in retrospect say,

That it had no place in the annals of fashion,

Other than a look that has now been rationed

To a space on a timeline

Where we compare and say,

"Now we are fine,

But look at that mistake, what a waste,

Not to mention a complete lack of taste."

But nonetheless, continue to profess

That the look of now is somehow different

And viable from now on.

As the designs are coming faster than fast

So soon to say that now is long gone,

And then to look at a wardrobe

Filled with so much skill but without care, beyond

And the audacity to say, "What to wear?"

To feel a need to prepare

For a cycle not called,

But planned to be pawned.

32

MY FRENCHNESS

I'm about as French as a

Wedge of brie, melted on a

Fried chicken leg,

Smothered in salsa fresca

Topping a bagel crusted pizza.

I'm about as French as an

Orthodox Rabbi reading

From the Quran on

Easter Sunday, amidst

The ruins of a Mayan temple,

Whilst clutching a photo of Stonehenge.

I'm about as French as

Mickey Mantle's New York Yankees jersey

Draped over the bough of a Maple tree,

Potted in the trunk of a '57 Cadillac El Dorado

On display amongst the Renaissance works

Housed in the Louvre.

I'm about as French as a shot of tequila,

Quickly imbibed while riding a crepe paper float

Adorned with a thousand Mermaids,

On the 17th day of March,

Singing aloft to the top of our voices

"La Marseillaise", in memory of the storming of the

Bastille.

I'm about as French as a Haitian exchange student

In Montreal getting a tattoo of the Fleur de Lit

After being accepted to graduate school

At University Bellarmine in Louisville,KY.

I'm about as French as an HMO

Delaying access of medicine to a

40 plus hour a week Janitor's son,

Due to a pre-existing condition

Known as being a child in a working class family.

I'm about as French as a Napa Valley Merlot

Being sipped from a ceramic mug

While listening to a rendition of

"Champs Elysees" played by Chet Atkins

as I ink these words.

Je m'appelle Nicholas Leon LaFond.

I'm about as French as that.

33

GRAFFITI IN THE BATHROOM

I don't ask the mountain to move,

Just that I can climb it.

It is not to avoid the obstacle,

But to overcome.

Ignition

Now.

I've learned a lot

By reading between the lines

Of the writing on the walls

Of all those bathroom stalls.

A map of the mind

Of middle America

And coastal sociology,

A lesson in perception.

Graffiti on a mirror

Next to my reflection

Spells out an identity,

An opinion,

Ignorance, genius,

All of it bliss, as it is a kiss

Of recognition.

The beauty of a cognizant mind

In tune with new surroundings

Somehow familiar.

34

RELINQUISHED INHERITANCE

Black, bold faced, looking back.

No, looking first.

Initiating, or, instigating,

Evoking a message,

Maybe inner thoughts surfacing nervously.

No, I mean no harm, no ill intentions,

I shrug off any imposed legacy.

But the ghost still at times

Haunts my thoughts.

The turmoil, it's

Only an echo,

I fight it lowering my guard

To the outside world.

Muscles contract a suspicious look,

Maybe a pained smile,

All the while fighting lessons

Not agreed with for a long time,

Since free thought bloomed.

Words, words are all I have.

Oh wait, actions! Words and actions!

Yes! Those I have and thought!

Powerful tools,

Weapons if necessary,

But to build.

Build a new possibility and

Allow for free will,

An element forgotten

In the pursuit of unity.

Slander and blame not a bridge

But kerosene and flame,

Rendering to ash the possibility

Of eye meeting eye,

Compromise a wisp of smoke to vanish in gust of wind.

Cautious, no,

But well thought with tongue.

Fragile is the path to peace,

Peace with fellow woman, fellow man.

Peace with self a rocky trail but less delicate,

Peace between one and another,

That is the butterfly's wing.

So proclaim! Make known!

Ring forth with resounding truth!

Keep ear open and heart exposed,

Also a muscle that strengthens with use!

Walk with light foot and heavy purpose.

The air that occupies the places between us

Not a wall, but a window

To look through and see

We are not alone.

35

SHED YOUR PREJUDICE

See one,

See a person.

Good.

That's but the decoration

Of who they are,

Appreciate.

Find deeper than you see.

Shed your prejudice and wear it not again,

Your soul will see clearly,

True eyes wide.

The water breaks!

Your true perception born!

Learn truth, not lies

The hate is gone!

Teach by the way you live.

Live for yourself, live for all.

May courage be yours to face your enemies,

May courage be yours to face your friends,

And feel not afraid but a sense of

Challenge,

There is nothing to fear

But much to be considered.

There is a new path to carve.

36.

HIGH HORSE

Once I rode so fair a horse

Pure as the driven snow,

From high atop the equine perch

I could see those far below.

Of their deeds, faults and misgivings

I could tell them all I know,

But in those days I had no mirror

For myself, my eyes to show.

The horse was tall, stood in the clouds,

Never felt the falling rain,

From aloft I saw no shame

For my obstinance so vain.

A bolt of lightning struck one day,

From the horse I was thrown away

And fell upon a stack of needles,

Grasping for a bit of hay.

The ground was hard and unforgiving

Though not as much as I to me,

The air was cold, my body shivered

As well as those that I did see.

But in swept a warmth of recognition

That helped my trembling to subside,

I saw through the clouds,

The horse was a ghost

No human cavalier could ride.

37.

SONG ABOUT BOB DYLAN

Someone once called him a

Folk singer,

Someone once wrote of him in print,

An anarchist.

He's just a man, been called a poet,

He called himself a guitar player

I think.

38.

LIVING IN LEAN

Not a day late,

For all I have right now is time.

Much more than a dollar short,

Oh yeah, the other thing I have right now is debt,

But also a sunrise.

So easy it is when pockets are thick,

To let words of immateriality fall carelessly from our lips.

So ready we are for acid comments

To jump from our mouths

When we are living in lean.

The bright side,

An exercise of my resourcefulness and

A chance to actually see the world

Through eyes in a familiar, yet fresh situation.

Time to evaluate, where have I come from,

What have I learned, what have I

And what am I going to do with it?

Time to appreciate and recognize

My good fortune.

To all those whose generosity

Provides me food, shelter

And help through the desert,

I profess my gratitude, and

Say that not in a merely passing,

Or light intention of placating customs,

But in honest word and action,

I thank you.

Also, I make new discoveries

Relating to current situation

And enjoy the occurrences

I'm perceiving and learning from.

Self fulfillment doesn't pay bills, necessarily,

But that is not the point anyway.

I have come across an obstacle

I have to deal with.

Life continues and the resources available

For learning and dealing with

And day to day

Are constantly malleable,

Changing, new.

My experiences, I see,

Are my education and

My fortune.

39

LUNA

Is it merely cliché

Or something more

That draws me toward

This glowing orb?

This shining rock

Pulls seawater in blood,

Makes eyes grow wide,

Heart pound strong in chest

And forget the rest

Of duties and deeds,

As Vernal lusts

Thrust like weeds

Out into the beautiful night,

The moon.

MEMORIES OF THE LAST FULL MOON

Memories of the last full Moon,

How bright it was and close!

How inspired the people

Lucky enough to experience

That vast indigo and

Welcome contrast,

Luminous and wise, always remembered

Always remembered.

So soon the full Moon retired

After the wax and wane,

Anticipation…

When you see the true beauty

There are no thoughts of temporary,

Expiration…

Such a distant figure yet

So much a part of our world,

Earth…

But since we knew that full Moon last

Our future becomes brighter than our past,

Birth…

When unsure the Moon lit our path

Just enough that we'd not fall,

People…

The Moon shone it's light fairly

Not just on some but on all,

Equal.

41.

CLUTCHING AT SMOKESCREENS

Down in the dregs of the listless horde

The savants preach to the seething drones.

Zombies who don't know their state,

Ignoring their light to purchase their fate,

And all the trappings of success

Further their actions, move to regress.

But if they could see themselves

Not in mirrors, not displayed on shelves,

What a change they'd make

When they saw the false as fake,

And they could grab a hold

Of their fate, to be as bold.

42.

BROKEN DREAMS AND SCARED MACHINES

Blue and brown, the colors of the worker.

White, blue and red,

The colors of corporatism, with choking neckties.

The workplace, a graveyard

Of actors too far from Broadway or Hollywood

And Rock stars, dead from an overdose of obscurity.

Dreams and hopes,

While once provided

Sustenance and a reason,

Now those same dreams

And those same hopes are scars

Not quite healed.

An acceptance of the lifestyle of a cog.

Just a part of the machine,

And delusions of being important to

The mechanism.

The machine cares not for the worker,

Only taps their energy and passion,

Replacing them when they are faulty

And slow down "progress".

The worker, to the machine, is interchangeable.

For the 5 on top know

They will continue to consume at all cost.

Whether in use,

Or rusting on the unemployment line

In tears of fear, angst and betrayal while still,

Probably unknowingly or in denial,

Fueling that which cares for them not

And has proven so.

The workers power is their numbers

And also, their individuality.

The green grease that lubricates the machine,

Allowing it to work,

Is what the workers,

The people, possess

And it is vital

To the corporate machine.

They use it up quickly and without it

The machine would crumble.

They are aware of this, the 5 on top,

And it terrifies them.

43

TAKING A BREAK TO BEGIN

I'm taking a break from it all

So I can begin.

If I had a love at one time

I tell you, show yourself.

If I ever needed before,

At least now I noticed.

To start somewhere

Is to know.

A face in static place

Is nowhere to hang your arms,

And Popeye is my man

Because I am what I am,

As love is abundant

Though truth is not redundant,

Because how can we say

What we feel?

If all that we say is word upon page

Or thought within skull

But our action is null,

What claim can we make to love?

And to my brother,

If I've fallen please don't regret

The days we've spent,

Our past in all its splendor.

Misty-eyed memories

They will perhaps someday be,

And until then, repent not against honest life

But move forward

And make the love you want to see.

44

DOWN IN THE MOUTH

'TIL MIND'S EYE IS WIDE

Depression is a potent intoxicant,

Ability impaired and

Judgment compromised by self-doubt.

Your image of self is surrogate,

While life is felt endured

And joy is done without.

See the Moon!

It's no drug, no lunar opiate,

But a cold pale sober

That fills my soul and

Excites me with life.

How cruel at times it seems,

Our existence,

Like acid on Winter flesh, that

Burns hot,

But leaves you still

Cold,

Fuel for our resistance, beyond

Debating from society what

We are told.

The beauty of randomness,

How picturesque.

A natural deviation,

The honesty of chaos.

Order is all in your perception!

Happiness is not denial, but

Knowing you live your life in truth.

45

A ROOF OVERHEAD

It was cold last night

I was nearly numb,

But not so enough to avoid

The bite of the dark, empty, cold

Air

Feet searched the bed and

Musty, but appreciated blanket

For even a second of warmth, yet

None to be found.

Hints of sleep

Frequently interrupted

By cold reality.

Every time a pocket of warmth

Was at last discovered,

Frozen imperialism would invade

And conquer that moment of reprieve,

Installing in it's place a frigid reminder.

At last the morning arrives

And is enough reason to

Get out of bed.

It was cold last night,

I'm thankful to have been inside.

46

OURSELVES

Red drops on rooftops,

Wine blots calm stops.

Signs along lines we painted ourselves

And only our true life is put upon shelf.

So much mirror,

So much feeling hidden,

Sustain and remain

In a fog of disdain,

Merely because you assume.

At times I feel we are all an assumption,

No credit due to someone,

SOMEONE,

Because we are all too infringed upon

By the dark parts of our own insecurity.

So much misunderstanding,

So much love just assumed, again,

As aggression or transgression.

My soul bleeds out onto white, blue lines,

And to reality I feel foreign.

Why can't I,

Can't we,

Be something other than commodity?

Other than tax revenue,

Other than job placement percentage,

Other than

Of what life is expected,

And for us,

We do something else.

So delicate,

Frost meeting warm breath,

Meeting sunlight rising,

We are merely bodies, bodies occupied.

Symbiosis with true life beyond days,

Yet we shit on each other,

And no one is righteous.

My fingernails bleed

From digging for reason and hope,

Understanding and friendship.

Why are we so scared to just be?

Ourselves.

47.

NOTEBOOK

Pages turn under pen

And the time that passes

Reflects in the ink as it fades.

A history, so brief as a notebook

Filled with ideas, thoughts

And heart bleeding,

Mind moving,

Soul pouring out,

Leaf upon leaf until it is filled,

So heavy, so fragile, moving, mundane.

48

LOVE LIKE WATER

Knew it was to happen, the end,

From the beginning

But I had to start it, even though.

I had to start it even though I knew

From the way your body spoke,

The way you withdrew,

You I couldn't keep.

Time passed and realization showed

It isn't to keep that which we love,

No, if to keep means to hold in restraint,

The meaning is in mirrored desire,

Love given, love accepted

And the vague vulnerability

Of recognizing,

And giving blessing,

To the freedom of the soul

You once thought to possess.

Love is like water,

Not that it slips through your fingers

As you try to hold it,

But that it can't be held in hands.

It is all within you

And what makes you live,

A force that moves you

And not you that moves it.

49.

PHOTO

I have one picture left

On my camera,

One more souvenir.

So much beauty all around

I never noticed before

And the Sun is going down,

The Sun is going down.

Is that the end?

The Sun will set

But the Sun will rise.

Will the Sun rise for me?

The Sun rises for everyone.

But will I be the same tomorrow?

Will I be myself?

What is tomorrow going to be?

Many say they know

But they have never been.

One picture left but many before,

Am I happy with my photographs?

Am I happy with my today?

I have one picture left on my camera

But there's no need to save it,

Who knows how long the days light will last

And besides, beauty cannot be captured

It just is.

50

MY BED WON'T BE MY GRAVE

My bed

Won't be my grave today.

Even if I stay inside,

I'm still going out to play,

With a score of questions about last night

And a heart half full of pain.

But my body's warm and the choir in my skull

Sings a glorious refrain.

When angel's darts hit heavy hearts

A valentine's for shit.

Sometimes a stranger's smile every once in awhile

Is the best that you can get.

The scars

On my eyes and on my brain

From some things I've seen and some things I've done

Could leave a gory, blood red stain.

Though I've made my peace with many

Whom I know I've wronged

My guilty feelings still remain.

I won't say I've done my part, I've barely started,

Don't need a pat on my back yet.

The past is past, that's what I learned from

To live today and look ahead.

My bed won't be my grave today,

My bed won't be my grave today.

51

BEYOND THE BILLBOARDS (THERE IS TRUTH)

While the rats are sleeping in the trees

I have morning coffee on the patio.

These days I listen to the word on the street

Much more than I bother listening to the radio,

Wherever you are the reports are the same,

There is always a chance of rain.

Headlines read plain and mundane,

It's what is between the lines

That shows the state of the game.

All the ghosts of what we think that we know

Are wearing t-shirts of old T.V. shows.

In several years, you would think that we'd grow,

But we've been given dead seeds, and we reap what we

sow.

What good is an alma mater

When all it has taught us is to become fodder?

Making automatons of the sons and daughters,

It trains the lamb to love the slaughter.

Our opened mouths need only taste

That which we pull to our face.

And I don't want to carry

Bouquets with their roots toward the sky.

52.

BROKEN BOTTLE

A broken bottle on the ground

Somehow

Reminded me of

Home

A place I used to

Know,

But nowhere seems to fit

Right

No, nowhere

Seems to fit right now

Nowhere not

Right now.

Happiness and joy exist

Just ahead

At the next spot, the next idea,

The next happening,

But what of where you've been?

Memory tends to lend a longing

To anytime but now,

Hope for future seems a double edged mistress,

But what of where we are? Where we're at?

Do we consider that?

"The worst time of year to be here"

That's what I heard

Soon after I arrived

"No one goes outside."

But now, now that I am

Leaving,

The doors,

The doors are opened wide,

Yes, they're all opened wide

53.

PERCEPTION

A pocket is a useless appendage without an opening.

A pocket doesn't exist without an opening, space,

Nor does an opening exist without the rest

Of the pocket.

An absurd concept to think of the one

Without the other,

But all the more reason

To consider it.

Move the commonplace for a moment

To where it is out of kind to it's surroundings,

Just to see what ideas you formulate.

A period is a signal

That what preceded it has ended.

What a curious practice,

If you decide it so.

A tale is a series of events

From start to end,

And the end is where a tail is found,

So maybe all things come to an end

Not because they must, but

Because we are trained that it is so, therefore,

In conclusion?,

We choose to end.

A means to an end,

Does the end justify the means?

If the end truly is just that,

Then why would you,

And to what or whom would you justify anything?

A work in progress is valid,

Though at times, is more of an ending,

Rather than a progression.

A painter looking at a musician's notebook

Would probably not understand,

Neither a sculptor,

But in their finished works,

Anyone can tell you all about

Their version,

Or misconception,

Of the artist's intention.

A reflection of self from all sides of the equation,

Yet rarely in relation to the musings

Of the one who made the expression

That inspired such introspection from those who see the art,

While the artist sees the reaction,

And no one is wrong,

There is only perception.

54

A RANT ABOUT THE GOVERNMENT

The blood spattered banner.

There is red on our flag too,

Literally and figuratively.

Yet many of our founding fathers,

I guess our founding mothers were too busy being

oppressed,

Subscribed to "red" theories

Before such a notion or

Propagated idea was incorporated.

True patriots right?

The Model Americans right?

But times change with the help of

Revolution.

Revolution is the unlisted amendment!

Our foundation is built on the ruins

Of a formerly oppressive government,

Only to be replaced by

Another

Oppressive government.

And so on as the years went by.

Today we see an approved model of our leaders

And only when there is need to cover up

An untidy mess somewhere else,

Does the dirt on our elected or appointed

Or however some of them got there,

Officials get attention from the campaign contributing

And benefit reaping media,

In order to keep our eyes off of the news.

Sounds almost Stalinist to me.

It used to be funny, how our country's

"Humanitarian Efforts"

often occurred where an abundance of

Resources or Strategic Geography were located,

But now it's just obvious.

The more I find out about

How and why our government got to where it is,

I realize why older generations have trouble believing

In the youth who speak and act.

55

FIRST TIME IN BOULDER, CO

On 13th Street, between College and Pennsylvania Avenue,

On my first night ever in Boulder Colorado

A man was shot and killed.

When arriving to the scene, after the hasty murder occurred

I made light of the situation, not knowing the serious nature of

What transpired there only minutes before.

No sensitivity killed that man, no compassion dug his grave,

And the day next, when yellow tape was cleared

And the streets appeared the same,

No one seemed to notice or even care that now

Everything had changed.

The onlookers with necks of rubber

Stood and stared and gossiped with each other,

And the scene felt of a party built around a bar brawl's epitaph.

I made a joke about what I didn't know

And seniors of the ambiguity smiled and laughed.

What had happened?

This seems more serious than at first what I perceived

And at that moment, the truth I overheard

But still did not believe.

Could it be? That in such a den of discovery

And security that possibly

Life is not as carefree

As one might originally perceive?

The instinct of survival,

Long since tainted by the arrival

Of eyes in selfish hues painted,

And community is forgotten

As even the basic decency of mutual respect

Is thrown to wayside,

And from Square to Highway

Our ethics defect

As our cities reflect

The secret of our demise,

And now, will we open our eyes?

ROCKS

Rocks show the timeline,

Are some stained with blood?

Ages beyond my knowledge,

History a catnap for these ancient watchers.

Man is a blink of an eye

Despite all of our "advancements",

And still,

People haven't solved their problems.

Who knows if we ever will solve them all.

WESTING

Men, like broken down trains

Rusting on a Sunny day,

Are freckles on the shoulders of the highways.

Conceptions, some here and some there, are missed

And convention is now seen altered.

This great land, now exposed to my eyes

Has become even more obscure,

A beautiful mystery.

The landscape pours out

As an aqueous fabric,

The clouds hang low over the desert

In isolated floodings.

Mountains eject from

What seems nowhere,

Objecting to the monotonous peace of the plains.

Thoughts and perceptions, new and ancient,

A people disperse and reconvene.

As the Sun sets and silhouettes

Paint pictures that tug at memories,

The images made as the days light fades

Speak totally unto your soul.

From green inland to green inland

Just shy of shining sea,

To make a scene

In a scene, stirs up the catalyst

For a voyage already desired,

And if not anything but,

Was well worth it.

Sleeping on the couch of a city

Indefinitely,

Not definitely a new home

But a new place anyway.

The promised land, not made of the golden ore,

But a glowing aura provides possibilities

And experiences are the mother of muse.

One side or the other isn't the focus,

Just the place.

58

STUBBORN AND OBSTINATE

Did you ever stop to think

Maybe you've got it all wrong?

All of your morals, methods and ethics

Confused all along?

I'm not saying stop your fight

But question your direction.

Accept the fact that

You're not always right,

Stop transgression, no more oppression!

So involved with your cause

You overlook some major flaws,

Maybe you are the cause of

An adverse effect,

But rather than adjust

You stubbornly object.

You might get more accomplished if

You weren't so elitist,

Focusing on trivial non-consequence

Seems all too defeatist.

Strength in unity!

Unity through compromise!

Compromise through understanding.

59

MY NEIGHBOR, THE DOG

The dog who is my neighbor

Came to me barking from his door.

I wondered what could be his problem?

What was all his barking for?

I stood and thought about it

While attempting to ignore,

Then something became clear to me,

Though neighbors

We never met before.

What a travesty that I ignored

While he roared at me.

The next day I awoke

And I thought about that dog.

We never had much need to argue,

But now our picket fence

Was an angry fog.

So I tried to listen to him

But his bark seemed so absurd.

Then I looked him in the eye

And he said more than I ever heard.

What a way to learn someone else's side,

Nothing got burned

And nobody lied.

A picket fence is a symbol

Of how some think things should be,

But as we gaze upon that structure,

Do we miss what that symbol means?

The lines that have been drawn

Across the land on which we live,

Support the impulse of the take,

But not the wisdom

To foster the give.

What if the dog, the mouse,

The bird and the cat

Could one day eat from the same trashcan,

Imagine that.

POLITICAL VOLLEY

Politics, like tennis,

Volley back and forth,

Left to right.

Head moves side to side,

Realize you are saying "NO"!

When they start playing tennis

Vertically,

We might be making progress.

A BRIEF SYNOPSIS ON HUMANITY

Define right and wrong.

Now, try to convince someone

To believe the same thing.

If they do, fully, believe

Exactly what you have defined,

You have created a religion.

If they disagree with what you have said,

And neither of you is willing to allow

For a difference of opinion

Or point of view,

You have started a war.

62.

FAITH?

Isn't all faith blind?

Wouldn't it be trust otherwise?

63

I CAN SMELL THE BURNING OIL

The stink of mankind,

All their plastics and burning oil,

Industry that cares not for whom it serves,

Only that it serves to serve it's purpose.

Use everything up, wringing out the last

Beautiful breath of fresh air

And invigorating landscape

For the purpose of imposing

An unrequested, yet gluttonized

"Quality of life"

Seen before it exists,

Then made to seem necessity,

Merely from over inundation.

The emphasis to the

Stumbling, groping as if blind, public

Tells them in Motherly tones

Or fantastic pomp and parade

"You need... this",

And with dumb trust

The masses abide by the flicker,

The glossy print,

The redundant narrowness of broadcast,

And feed upon troughs of child labor,

Corner cut low quality,

Mass produced peak of

What has become thought of as

Capitalism.

Complaints are not now extinct,

Nor are the overworked and underpaid unmentioned,

And the grey air and brown water

And effected citizens

Have not been made clean and healthy,

Yet there is more opposition than agreement

To the idea that these are in need

Of remedy.

The gun was loaded by unchecked corporatism

And unapologetic industry.

It is we, the People,

Who hold it so firm against our temple.

64.

NEW ROME

The bitter words drip from their mouths,

Prophecies are truth when self fulfilled.

It's the reason they send the soldiers

Far from home,

Strangely self-proclaimed,

A demise preordained,

They call it New Rome.

And as I try to see across the hills,

The mountaintops strong and surreal,

The clouds, they hide the valleys below

Obscuring how far down they go.

Yet, of all we say we "know" of God,

What if the Lion of Judah was a dog?

Of all the righteousness of Allah's might,

Did Jahweh come and say who's right?

65

STARDUST

Tinkle, tinkle,

The sound of stars broken

And trust clatters as it is shattered on the ground.

At last we see the weight of the situation profound!

Citizenry bound and gagged

By American flags!

Old Glory mopping up messes, gory

And the truth obscured,

While we are all assured

By the Devil's disguise with beady little eyes.

Would Satan even commit deeds so terrible?

We need educators!

Where's Manning Marable?

Professing parables, so enabling minds

To see clear, think free,

And in the hour of need,

We notice follies of greed

At the same time saying, "God speed"

With a slap on the back

As boys and girls are sent off to attack

A people angry, rightly so,

Imagine if militias destroyed your home.

The terribles of the past

Are characters cast

On dictators of today

So Pres can say ,"We fight the good fight",

Yeah right, bet you wouldn't bomb them

If they were Christians and white.

Squinty ocular with short sight, no vision,

Not so popular world wide for current decisions,

Making incisions, carving a line

In the sand to make arrogant demands

On friends, or so they thought,

But peace was bought by unified trade

And you can see that without Sam Spade

To detect, yet still

The citizens see no need to object?

The media is a weapon against us!

Thrust us into heated situations

No one trusts U.S.

So they are against us?

Called a terrorist when you make a fuss

About a pimple tense situation ready to bust

And spew puss

On the mirror of safety.

It's the last month on our lease on peace,

Which is a farce,

And we blame it on cars?

No.

The vote, the referendum!

We never sent them notice of discontent,

Just expressed vengeful pro-war sentiment.

Signing over our freedom to an unelected President

Wanting to set precedent

By destroying all Middle East residents.

Here's a bag of pretzels, go take a nap

And shut your yap,

Breath reeks of shit from talking so much crap!

Snow nose for no doze

Looked at as a hero,

Do you play the fiddle or should we call Nero?

Because you're gonna burn the empire you want to build,

I'm not saying anyone should be killed,

But I would be thrilled

If you were gone after next election!

Cleaned out like Neosporin on an infection,

Merely for Our protection.

Without another day of infamy

Will we ever learn our lesson?

No more war desire,

Be forward pressing.

66

PRIVILEGE AND PREJUDICE

A hardheaded soldier

In a war with no sides

Idly marches through a sea of people,

Blind and full of pride.

He's got no conception

About living on this Earth,

Just feels that he's entitled

And has been taught that since his birth.

And can you blame the dame who held him

Closely to her breast?

Raised him on the family milk

Taught him whom he should detest.

Within all of her preaching,

Teaching about who is the best

It never occurred to him

That he should protest,

So long as he can close his eyes

And keep his conscience neatly pressed.

Daddy's money is good

But Mommy's money is better,

Because Daddy's cash come with a guilt trip and judgment

But Mommy's just comes with a letter,

And Mommy knows perfection

Is exactly what she has made,

While Daddy's still wondering

When Baby is going to get paid.

His perception of People in his day to day

Is that all who with him don't

Praise and agree,

Are merely obstacles in his way.

Never worked a day

Yet he walks in new shoes,

His soft hands never tip

And from his lips to the servants

He gives only abuse.

What can you tell someone

Who feels they know it all?

You can struggle with lipstick

And crayons and spray-cans

And try to write on the wall,

But to the likes of him, that won't prove nothin',

Just colors your hands to be caught.

He would let you be thrown in a cell to rot

And about that he'd be not stressed,

So long as he can close his eyes

And keep his conscience neatly pressed.

Take a day away from yourself

Have a stroll in the shoes of someone else

And if after the Sun's rise and set,

And after the Moon has dipped into the West,

Come talk to me if you're still feeling

That you're above the rest

And I will peel away your armor,

Even though you might protest,

And leave with nothing but

The best I can suggest.

67

LILIES FOR OUR TROUBLE

A field of lilies, no hothouse flowers,

Grow them up right, to be put to use.

Arrogant hateful, would have lives thrown away,

No balances or checks

A vengeful god complex.

Black blood drips now slow,

Making the blue blood boil,

Words reflect compassion, but there is no compassion.

Defense through invasion

And now the lilies are in bloom,

They'll spare life no expense,

One bloom for every tomb.

Ghost chasing,

A haunted past remains,

Make room on the wall

To etch a thousand more names.

Meanwhile sanctions kill

More children every day,

Advertised to eyes ignore sad truth,

People dying, embargoed youth.

Human rights, a smoke thin alibi.

Atrocities reflect back a leader with no eyes.

No concept of remorse,

Mouth drips in want of blood.

Such desire for destruction,

Their solution is the problem.

Foresight is a myth

In the midst of bloodlust leadership.

The media as the Whitehouse concubine

Aims to please, on your knees,

Forget your needs,

Turn on your T.V.

Justify the deeds.

They only show us

What they want us to see.

Marching blindly towards our fate,

But our fate is what we make.

The flood is levee high, how long before it breaks?

Restraint seems lost, world waits with baited breath,

World's weight on shoulder,

So much for one to heft.

No trust for one whose sole concern is self,

Whose motivation is for power and wealth,

Who believes the cost of lives is worth

Global dominance,

But loss of Earth.

68

THE DAWN

The night comes and I step out of the door.

My breath floats through the Autumn chill.

The heavens are alive, all Stars and Moon,

And all seems wonderful as a dark cloud looms.

Downtown all things are hustle and move.

People kiss, people fight, some people think they've

something to prove.

Most folks have got so much on their minds,

Everyone looks at the clock but they don't notice the time.

As vengeance rears its head again,

His judgments passed on imposed sin,

He says "retaliation" and gets applause

But what's retaliation when you're the cause?

Morning comes and something happened last night,

Besides the noise besides the sex besides all the fights.

A decree came down ex post facto

And left us standing with a big bag to hold.

It's about time we choose for ourselves!

Do we know what we want? Then why leave it to someone

else?

Sunset comes and unfurls the night again.

Nothing really looks different, but I feel a change.

Awareness was asleep, but now it's out of bed

And telescopes aimed at bedroom walls are now aimed at

stripes and stars instead.

Now I see we can see the dawn.

PEACE ON THE PRECIPICE

Situations so tight

It's hard to think,

For the mind to breathe,

The tension won't leave

And the bridges are soaked with kerosene!

The vulture holds peace in its beak.

MARCH OF THE HYPOCRITES

Rat tat tat, the drum,

Rat tat tat, the drum,

Rat tat tat, we wish to bring the world our freedom.

Rat tat tat, it goes,

Rat tat tat ,it goes,

Rat tat tat, our lifestyle we impose.

Rat tat tat, the guns,

Rat tat tat, the guns,

Rat tat tat, opposition better run.

Rat tat tat, we won!

Rat tat tat, we won!

Rat tat tat, how red the setting sun.

FOREIGN POLICY BLAST

Exporting small pox

While words and gestures

Blanket domestic

Ears and eyes.

BATTLEFIELDS

I look out on the fields of the

Battles I've waged

And they all seem so trivial,

They just fade to gray.

The Sun and the Moon used to matter so much

I guess they still do,

It's just that to me

My skin doesn't feel like me anymore,

I forgot about what I was fighting for.

The meaning, it fell

From the table to the floor.

No angels did cry, they just passed me by.

So much to do, but all I do is say

I thought I might be a hero in some way,

But I don't know how to save the day.

I look at the people I see everyday,

Sometimes their faces,

They all look the same.

I looked like a drowned rat while caught in the rain

Someone once told me,

Seems so long ago.

The fields are now growing with grass once again

And the battles I've waged have left behind scars.

Those who have fallen are of hopes and doubt,

They are my history,

I have learned from them well,

I will remember them well.

Words, they come quick but seem wasted.

What of this life have I tasted?

What do I know of the ebb and flow?

Only footprints and notebooks

Filled to the brim.

Lucid daydreams, they come and they go,

It's hard doing today

While living for tomorrow.

All I have is today.

73.

YOU ARE NOT A COLOR

You are not a color.

You are not a gender.

You are not a sexuality.

Those are conspiracies,

Fostered and cultivated by those

Who would have you under their control.

Brands put on you like packaging,

A serving suggestion of who you are,

Easy for people to see, and

Easy for people to disregard or assume familiarity.

Product placement, to make sure

The idea of one side of track mingling with another,

Or even obliterating the tracks altogether,

Is rendered incapable of occurrence.

You are a living, breathing, seeing, hearing, eating, shitting, smiling,

Fucking, singing, feeling, contemplating, reeling,

Raging, moving, doing, not-doing,

Touching, caressing, working, wanting,

Knowing, not-knowing,

Starting, stopping, having, not-having,

Loving being,

Being led around by target market research,

While intelligence and sensitivity are

Insulted, slapped across the face.

The labels that have usurped

We, the People, remember?

Are for those too lazy

To attribute an individual unto themselves,

Instead finding ease in the comfort of

Sweeping generalizations

As they wonder why

They don't know their own self.

Identity of self is not uniformity,

Not for everybody,

Maybe not for anybody

Despite recent trends reported

Of one cola matching a pair of shoes in the Midwest

Or wherever.

You are not a color.

You are not a gender.

You are not a sexuality.

You are an individual,

Your only label your name

And that,

Is what you do with it.

74

HISTORY'S NEW PAGE

Taken from home,

Bribed out from your home,

Home was taken away

Taken from your home,

Pushed out of your home,

Home was taken away

Lies destroyed

Eyes saw

Unequal

Betrayed by those you saved

Virus as a gift

Not from a god

Greed, a civilized disease.

Would things be changed

If friends were made

Not homeschooled enemies?

The past can't change

But new history becomes

The teacher of the next age

So much to say

But easy to start,

Free minds and equal eyes.

75.

HER PLEASURE IS PAIN

A kiss that tastes like whisky not wine

Nails down the chalkboard,

Bloody shivers up my spine.

Hugging wrists below clenched fists

Lips are bitten but not to resist,

Some pain in the love,

Some bitter fruit on the vine.

She closes the blinds, bright shine the stars,

The pain, she don't mind, she's fine leaving scars.

She says, "It's true, we've all got some.

You don't like it, you don't want more

Then honey, don't come.

You and I are not yours or mine

But the pain we make is ours."

She may be a Venus,

But she can be just as mean as Mars.

Her body doesn't quit, it's posture wryly smirking.

I can't tell if she's in love with me

Or if she's in love with the working.

It's nor her job though she does it so well

Who knew giving pleasure could hurt like hell.

Never in her lovers arms

When they are handcuffed to the bedpost,

It may not sound like a true romance

But from what she gets she makes the most.

You and I are not yours or mine

But the pain we make is ours.

She may be a Venus,

But she can be just as mean as Mars.

Some pain in the love,

Some bitter fruit on the vine.

76.

RADIO TODAY

People

What you listenin' to,

These grooves are flat.

You call it pop,

I say, then where the fizz at?

You say,

"Yo man, it's the shit"

and you're right at that,

The radio today

Is so lame

It's the shit that shit shat.

77

HARMONY AND UNISON

The mundane is immediate

And so obvious is survival,

Our biology dictates our society

And greed keeps us there.

Be it ours

Or the trickle down greed of others

Accepting the "rule of life",

Born, school, college, work,

Desperation or mid-life-crisis

And then death,

All at the hands of "the almighty",

The dollar god

Of our society's existence

And we,

Out of fear and desire

For the cult of commerce,

Bow down and

Submit our freedom

To the cost of doing business.

One voice alone gets attention

A choir of voices makes action.

78.

MAN VS. NATURE

The ducks fly

In formation or randomness,

In unison or

Individually

Together,

They skim the

Upside down shimmer

Of the manmade lake

And have all the space in the world.

Humans, being arrogant

And usually superficial,

Think they know what's

Best for nature

So they destroy

One habitat for another.

Nature

She is strong.

She will be here long after

We have destroyed

Ourselves,

Or been destroyed,

Perhaps by nature.

WHAT WE SAY

It's just writing,

They're just words.

What is said?

Does it reflect

What it is that we want to say?

Do we say anything at all?

SO MANY DANCES, SO MANY REASONS

A measure.

A measure of what, a man?

4 beats to claim redundant

If you really listen,

But more for purpose of dancing,

Around subjects, around truth, around the room.

Watch whom you step on, over,

The eyes! Don't look!

Lest you have to admit.

Admit what?

Dancing…dancing…dancing.

Boom, thump…boom, thump…boom, thump…boom,

thump,

The beat so attractive

So irresistible

It is biological,

The logic of life.

The measure,

The measure of a man? Ha!

What a laughable truism.

It seems a shame to place that limit

On yourself or someone.

Dancing, it feels good,

If you don't do it once in awhile

You're missing out.

The liquor tastes like vomit.

Why bother?

What would we do without it?

Without that social safety net? Hmmmm...

Dancing,

An excuse to release deep hidden information

About ourselves, freely for some.

A casual bounce hides

A powder keg of explosive gyrations,

Arms flailing, beautifully, true,

Allow, it feels good.

No ruler.

How do you measure that which

You can't, or choose not to define?

Dancing,

Between sadness, joy,

Hinting towards ecstasy or rage,

Helpless to hopeful.

81.

THE WORLD AS WE SEE,

WE ARE FREE IF WE LIVE FREE

It seemed my joy left with a snowfall,

Or at least snow was falling

When I noticed it's fleeting.

Now, again, it is snowing or sleeting,

I wonder if my joy will come back.

Is it meant to be?

Or am I just scrutinizing my luck

Once again, as I have noticed

Lately is an often occurring theme.

Now though,

I've been able to realize

That I'm not alone in my occasional anguish,

And that I should spend more time on empathy

And effort, rather than underlying themes

Of feeling pathetic.

There are many possibilities and

My attitude is what can make or break situations,

So my destiny is changeable

And up to me.

Enough self pity,

I renounce it

Because it is so frivolous compared to

The needs of so many other problems,

And so many people in myriad states of

Trouble and despair.

From a skinned knee

To a distant love,

To a loved one's passing

To a people whose lives and culture are

In urgent peril.

A motion for emotional strength

And a movement for compassion for

Our fellow people.

We are all equal despite our differences,

Of origin and opinion and intention.

My problems?

Some are valid, but more insignificant

In the greater spectrum.

Now, let's start living

And shed our feelings of non acceptance

That keep us held back

By no one but ourselves.

We are free if we live free.

82

A BLURRED PHONE # ON A COCKTAIL NAPKIN

In the dregs of the party,

The running mascara,

The spent,

The blurry back seat of the taxicab,

In the bitter taste or the sweet smile,

Of not knowing what the fuck you're talking about,

That's where the most education is in the experiment.

You learn your limitations and some continue to defy them.

You learn the face of paranoia.

Trust is still earned, yet a hotter commodity than ever

before

Or since.

"Why" is answered with another night out

Chasing things you say you don't want.

Vomit, worn like a badge of honor

To impress who?

Intimacy becomes a solitary activity while emotions

Are hidden and conscience is kicked

To the side, balled up on the floor, to be collected

In the early morning light with the hope

That with a washing, it will be clean again.

Innocence lost? No,

Merely remembered, but gone all the same.

I say this not from a self righteous pulpit

Or a high and mighty soap box, but from

A point of view reflecting upon experiences and neon

From nights and mornings

And day to day,

That have passed

And that continue.

For the most part we know the answers to our own

questions,

We allow our misery,

We allow our happiness

And it's all very simple.

83

THOUGHTS ON ANARCHY

Oh say what you see!

And accept that you might be wrong.

Winning and losing are all in

The angle of inspection,

I think of Clarence Darrow.

Not for battling a faith

But for opening the eyes,

Minds of some, the doors for others,

As free thought was the rush of children to recess

From the classroom of a fundamentalist oppression.

A trial lost maybe,

A victory won for sure.

Not to use law for self-service, lip service, face time,

But to enjoy the right to help others

Move towards communal theory,

Recognizing that community can be, and is better

When made up of individuals,

As that is what we are.

But to deny the right of folks to be also individuals

Is to negate our own right to self,

In self righteousness.

Less of that I say,

More recognition and embracing of differences

Where political ideals can be discussed,

Even heatedly,

Without any wish or inkling of want

To harm one for differing in opinion.

Recognizing opinions for what they are, opinions,

And realizing that facts are also subject to perception

At times.

An absence of Government

With a responsible, communal,

Self governed population?

A fantasy maybe,

But an element within our situation to consider.

Am I right? No.

Am I wrong? No.

Am I thinking?

Yes.

84.

MY HANDS AMONGST THE OTHERS

I'm pulled

Back and forth, back and forth

Against the grain.

I'm tied in knots,

Stretched tight,

They ignore the tension

To the point

About to snap.

No solace in relaxing,

Makes me restless.

So much to do

No time, but it's all I've got, all I've got

And it seems it's not enough.

Is there something to keep me sane

As I cope with what feels like psychosis?

And the knife twists in back and in front,

With my hands amongst the others.

But now I've pulled it out

And thrown it on the ground,

No more lack of confidence

To keep me down,

And I know the negative still exists

But I will focus on the positive,

Not on what I've missed.

85

RAGE

I could just go into the grocery store and

Rip the produce shelves down.

I could jump off of the deck

And land on my chest.

I could destroy things with the

Intensity of my anger,

Rend things to broken

Because of the ferocity of my emotions,

Ruin something beautiful

Just because

That's not how I feel,

Or, I feel that is something I can't have.

What a strange emotion,

At once disgusting, perhaps even frightening,

And then again

So pure and true,

Rarely does one lie about their rage.

To feel rage is at times unavoidable,

But does not require one to act in anger.

86.

OH BUFFOON, MY BUFFOON

So sad to see another hateful man

With such influence in his hands.

Like sowing seed on sand,

No progress in his mind,

Spending much but wasting time.

Blind flying towards a goal

Undetermined, undefined,

Undermined by lack of support

Which is all he has earned,

And learned nothing

But to try harder not to get caught,

Accept no blame,

Hold no fault.

87

RED LINE

Red line.

From point "a" to point "b",

Showing travel,

Showing distance.

We see distance as accomplishment,

We see distance as heartache,

We see distance as safety,

We see distance as difficulty.

Distance is married to longing or goal,

A finite curriculum to gauge life in vignettes.

Red line.

A warning, a separation, a border.

A rule, a security blanket, an obstacle.

We are shown where not to go

Based on a consensus of others,

Most of whom never bothered to cross

And, for themselves see.

We stay away from dangerous interactions,

Some trepidations valid but most cast unjustly.

A name, an identity,

Merely association based on geography

And imperialist ideals, antique and modern.

A law written by few

To control many.

Comfort for those who believe the hype

And are frightened into compliance,

A hassle for the ones

Who choose to point out the fact that

They do not concur.

Red line.

Life represented by its physical nectar.

A pact between friends.

An early sign of responsibility.

A trail of evidence.

A sign of attempt to live.

A show of disdain for life or situation.

Spilled out in play by accident,

In anger or aggression,

Incisions to repair, incisions to destroy another,

Or self, a burden? A joy? Merely genetic?

Or for a reason?

A red line.

A red line.

A red line, awash in color.

88

MS. CHAMOMILE CHILE

She was a girl,

Offered a nervous smile, with beauty brown eyes,

Ms. Chamomile Chile.

I'd sworn off women, out of respect, for a little while

And she thought so much of me,

Ms. Chamomile Chile.

I'd seen her grow up,

As I did too,

Noticing her groovy style,

An interesting girl I thought to myself

Young Ms. Chamomile Chile.

Some years occurred and to me,

High school been gone for miles,

She out a year or two, grown up a young woman,

Why hey there, Ms. Chamomile Chile.

So shy she was and to her it seemed a trial,

Just to get the courage to ask me over,

Nervous Ms. Chamomile Chile.

And I would come over,

We would walk and talk

All as tension compiled,

Yet at the end of the night

Or in days first light,

Home I went,

Sorry Ms. Chamomile Chile.

Now I've never been,

When it comes to women,

A man of suaveness or guile,

But this lady, for me,

Had an aching heart it seemed,

Forlorn Ms. Chamomile Chile.

Her friends would tell me,

As did her feminine wiles,

And I played distant or dumb

And tried to be numb,

What's that Ms. Chamomile Chile?

Why did I sidestep your feelings

And keep your embrace at denial?

Why, when you made me feel good,

Why Ms. Chamomile Chile?

Because I knew I was leaving

And didn't want to put you on file,

I wanted to do you right, or not at all,

That's truth Ms. Chamomile Chile.

So if ever you read this,

Your anger I don't wish to rile,

Don't take this the wrong way,

I guess I still think of you today, but,

Thank you Ms. Chamomile Chile.

89.

THE SHADOWS, REMAINS

Can't you see the shadows?

Can't you see the shadows?

The charred remains

Can't you still see the shadows?

Since one method is flawed

You decide on destruction,

You haven't even tried!

There is more money in death

More expense in life.

Selfish prick

You don't even seem to care

That if not you,

Your children will suffer from

Your shortsighted tyranny.

5,000 pounds

A weight you shrug without remorse,

What are you fighting for

If your goal is complete destruction?

You wave a flag of justice

As we learn of your corruption and greed,

You claim this is for freedom,

Redundantly,

While you destroy our rights

Like so much collateral damage.

I

don't

agree

with you.

90

ORPHANS OF CULTURE

Faces told stories in a day,

Told of times.

Ancients and contemporaries

Had a home,

Now, just a place.

What is forgotten is not the time

But the meaning,

Just the reason.

Harmony lost,

No longer dissonance.

Only melody

For the sake of one,

And only one.

Orphans of culture

Screaming for nothing at all.

No sound for anything,

No noise for our time.

91.

SPECIMEN

Angelic caress,

My cheek

But I don't

See her there.

Speak in glimpses,

Life is dulled.

I taste the world

At my feet,

Removed

From consciousness

The world seems foggy

But sweet and gray.

Social apathy

Is welcomed happily,

It's such a travesty

A pill for amnesty.

92

CONVERGING LINES

The cloth that covers my eyes,

I can see through,

I can see through what I'm given to see.

The glass is painted with facts,

Most are untrue save syntax,

"Shut up and buy it, shut up and buy".

More truth is found in comic strips

Than in fashion magazines,

The news is for the benefit of corporate machines.

When leaders are sold like a product line,

My conscience won't relax and tell me

Everything is fine.

Headlines come to us all pre-chewed,

Artificially flavored brain food.

Crime and punishment advertising

To keep us all from realizing

That if we talk to our neighbors,

And step out of our doors,

We can live in *our* neighborhoods

And be afraid no more.

There is truth in front-page news

But it lives between the lines, between the lines.

Diamonds and blood are thrust at us

To distract our watchful eyes,

To keep attention and our questions averted

From 5 converging lines.

With eyes open and ears to the ground

We can smell what's going on,

Beneath the surface of the Earth

There are forces going strong.

We are satellites of what we hold dear,

Distorted truths have our societies eyes glazed

But we can break through the veneer,

And sever the tether that tightly binds

The albatross to the freedom

Of our bodies and minds,

Destroy the castles we have built for them

Throughout time

And bring about the end of

The 5 converging lines.

93

FEET, DON'T FAIL ME

The feet in my shoes are mine,

They take me where I want to go.

They are long and thin, but that's fine,

Though I've tripped, they never failed me before.

And the places I've been, the places I will go,

It's because of them and because of more,

It's something within that keeps my feet on the road,

It's a blessing and a sin

That I've been praying for.

If we were roads, what would destinations be?

Would occurrences be travelers

Making their way across us?

Or would we just be scenery?

The dust could be our sweat

Stirred up from passers by,

Who may or may not forget

What they saw on this drive.

The space in my head is mine.

It's filled with what I call my mind.

It's been known to be cruel,

It's been known to be kind,

Depends on whom you ask

And at what time.

Sometimes I feel that I should charge rent

For all the time that's been spent

By you, yes you know who you are,

Trying to hold onto the snowflakes

And the stars.

Of all we've been given,

How much do we receive?

And after everything we've been shown,

How much do we believe?

Where will you ever stay if all you do is leave?

How can you deal with sadness

If you never take time to grieve?

Along the way? Along the way

Is where we find ourselves,

Is where we live!

Along the way, along the way.

94.

PRICE PER OUNCE

The value of Gold

Comes from its likeness

To the Sun

And our want of it.

But Icarus tried

To touch the Sun

And fell to his death

For his Father's arrogance.

And we,

Our society,

Scramble and lie

While our ethics and people

Die

All with their eyes

Toward the "Sun".

95

FROM THE ASHES OF DISASTER

I'm feeling like a loser

I'm feeling like a shithead

And I'm wondering why I'm wasting breath

On words already said.

I'm sitting on the couch now

Idol on the screen is glistening

And I ask myself why I am sitting

Just watching what I am missing,

Watching while I'm missing.

A tortured soul making his own pain,

A slave holding his own chains,

A zombie eating his own brains,

A gravedigger burying his own remains.

And I ask, what challenge am I seeking?

Of self loathing I'm reeking!

At what point do I tear down the curtain

Instead of 'round it merely peeking?

From behind it never peaking.

I guess I will grab a pair of scissors

Gleaming, shining, sharpened, glistening

And sever the tethers I use to hold me back,

Speaking while I'm listening

Yes speaking, saying but also

Listening.

Building a tribe from the son of a bastard,

The servant now has become the master.

After a broken bone the healing comes faster,

A new life born from the ashes of disaster.

I can see myself without a mirror

By looking at the way I'm thinking.

I've realized I'm the only one over me who has control

I can stare into myself without blinking!

And I've stared into myself without blinking.

So I picked up my guitar and started playing.

I wrote some words and now I'm singing!

My mind, my heart, my soul are out upon the table

And through them my voice is ringing,

Shining brightly they all are ringing.

I was a tortured soul making his own pain,

A slave holding his own chains,

A zombie eating his own brains,

A gravedigger burying his own remains.

But now I'm building a tribe from the son of a bastard,

The servant now has become the master!

After a broken bone the healing comes faster,

A new life born

From the ashes of disaster.

96

WINE AND GUITAR

I've got my wine and my guitar.

Through a midnight, flailing,

The star's light shows my scars.

And though the woman's life was saved,

My love landed in the grave.

The love that's left is in my head,

But not my heart.

And what more could I expect?

What I thought I had was never in my hands.

The lesson was tough indeed

And it left me there to bleed,

But now I know.

True love is not to have or to hold,

It's the warmth in the middle

Of the cold.

My memory knew her,

But her love she hadn't shown.

I couldn't sit there dreaming

Of our some day happy home.

Now that dream is gone,

I woke up and moved on.

And I must admit,

Yeah, I must admit,

I've gotten good at being alone.

Yeah, I've gotten good at being alone.

97

PARENTAL ADVISORY

A child seems so young

And then, so do his parents.

It makes me think

About when I was that age,

Old enough to know and

Young enough to not worry

Of remembering.

Were my parents that young?

Watchful eyes hint at

A protective manner,

Over protective even.

Better than using T.V. as

Nursemaid and then

Enforcing punishment

For rules broken,

Though not explained

Or even fully declared.

They wonder why

The evening meal is so quiet

And why the child plays their stereo

So loud.

"Why do they wear so much black?"

A question in syntax,

But more an indirect reprimand

And not an effort to understand

A person they realize they don't know,

A stranger of same blood,

Bless the family unit,

Amen.

A PHOTOGRAPHIC MEMORY

A photograph is just a memory.

Stare and stare and stare at it

But it won't come back,

It won't come back.

What's done is done,

The good and bad,

You can't count on things being the same

Again.

THE LIGHTER SIDE OF DARK

When all seems like

Darkness,

Even the smallest light

Can be easier seen.

Not all darkness is to escape

It sometimes is the comfort sought.

Darkness and light,

Which one shines brighter when

One shines for hate,

But ones dark is full of their love.

Light reveals truth mostly

With vision,

Dark reveals truth to those

Unafraid to feel.

To rely on light to see

Is to be blind half of the time,

Learn to see through

The light and the dark,

See beyond the outside and

Know

That sometimes,

The simple

Is all that is there,

Like day or night.

100

STRANGER AT A PARTY

So many unfamiliar faces

That look like someone I know,

Far away from this place though.

Or maybe not,

Maybe they are

In the same place

Just somewhere else,

Seeing my face in someone else.

Attitudes and personalities are

Also found to be not similar

In the most basic ways,

With an occasional glimpse

Of complexity.

And sometimes

There are great conversations,

Conversations! Not just talking!

And sometimes

I'm even involved

In these wonderful conversations!

Then, as I glide home

Over sheets of ice, amidst crisp air,

The beautiful Moon shines upon me.

Did I say home?

What I meant was

Hmmm…

NEW IN TOWN

Pardon me for a second,

But I guess your two cents

Is worth more than a penny for my thoughts

Well… free.

But hey,

What's your name

In this game,

In this game

You pretend does not exist,

Yet you are of the many

Players,

You,

Antagonist.

SWEET BLUE EYED GIRL

A beautiful person, though

I realize we've met just a few times.

I know her only through what I

Have perceived.

Were there such a thing as perfect,

Close to it she would be.

Yet still, the need I feel

To ask her, "are you happy?"

Sometime, someplace,

Maybe, could, would,

When and why not…

She should know how I feel,

But to say it I refuse.

I would only be an interruption

So it stays inside

As I chalk it up to muse.

Heart not broken

Though when I speak to her I stammer.

But no pain,

The anvil of my affection has not been pounded

By the denial of her hammer.

Why hold inside

Honest feelings?

Why not make known?

Testify, be bold!

I have something to say,

I think I'm in love with you.

103

THE SENSATION OF FALLING

Falling from a cliff

Did I slip or dive?

Don't know how deep is the water

Will I survive?

If I live through the fall

Then I will have to swim.

Will I remember how

To move my limbs?

Enough! Enough of this talk, talk, talk!

The time is now!

Make your fate!

We are the life we are looking for,

Let motivation lead to action!

So many thoughts run through my head

In such a short amount of time,

Clearing all insecurity

From my mind.

Gravity's effects

Pull me towards a place,

Obstacles and adversity

I may have to face.

Fear is not a part

Of the vision that I see,

My will must be stronger

Than the depth of uncertainty.

Not grasping for a branch

To save me anymore,

I prepare to hit the water

And swim to shore.

At last! At last we can see we are able!

Action from motivation! Motivation from action!

No more am I held back,

I know I can achieve!

There is nothing out of reach!

104

TO NAME A BAND

I could have called it Jesus' Son

In all that falsehood, besides,

It's been done.

Might as well call it

"What's In A Name",

Not as a question,

But a quest just the same.

Planes mistaken as ghosts on high

Playing tricks, my mind on my eyes.

Then remembering it's all for fun

And those who have fought, all,

Are who have won.

New wet upon old sweat,

Target for creative or negative epithets,

Asphalt the skyway

No budget for jets,

Awake in the dream

No hedging of bets,

Too verdant to think of that "yet".

No need to plunge into that net.

The time is what's spent

Because it's all that's got,

Payback's a bitch

When you don't care for what you bought.

Tactless mouths spew checks that bounce

Straddling struggling shoulders

To grasp at coats,

The measure, living gold,

Valued per ounce,

The rest can rot, cared for not,

Wait to pounce…

And not just cream floats.

What's inside that counts?

Rain washes away

And Sun dries the Rain,

Both necessary, a balance to maintain.

Ritual upon tradition

More as time has passed,

Cracks in cement eroding wide and vast,

But head and heart remember more

Than injuries and wounds

From days of yore.

105

A LOOK AROUND THE ROOM

AND OUT THE WINDOW

The words tumble through,

Wishes for my heart to pour

From pen to page,

The ink flows so smoothly,

No matter where she hears this

She will know it's for her.

Fantastic is the word she has named me

Too many times today. I feel unworthy.

The cat upon the windowsill is a lover

Who fights catfights with his brother

And the moon near full

Leaves us with a gesture

To the sun's steady gain.

If she knew what she held,

The world at her open palm.

Forever she is embraced in loveliness,

As flowers and plumes escape her bosom's pull.

She knows,

And it's just a song from the soul of a martyr.

She claims a love for one

Who knows, his time in her eyes

Will come to a close

And his garden more beautiful

From the tears he may sow.

106

OPPONENTS OF FREE SPEECH (AND HEROIN)

KILLED LENNY BRUCE

His world was wider since he sailed the sea

And coming home it seemed that he

Had found a voice and they'd come to see,

Or watch him shine on their T.V.

A star was born.

A star is born, a star is born,

In crowded sky he shined alone.

They loved the child, though he was grown

For the jokes he told of the world he's known.

Canonized and given throne,

Wife and child, a happy home,

A star had grown.

The powers that were and continue to be,

Stole his throne and said the he

Could no more speak his mind as free

Under their reign of tyranny.

Wife and child gone, his life was bleak

And the poison made him weak,

A star got burned.

The law would hound him where he would roam,

Still he fought nail, tooth and bone.

His eyes were distant, his smile had flown,

Had he forgot the humor he'd known?

In some motel room

Where he died alone,

The morning headlines of the paper shone,

A star was blown.

A star was born, a star had grown,

A star got burned, a star was blown.

A DOSE OF LITERARY TOURETTES

Streetcar Named Desire!

I don't desire to ride you.

Why have I been seeing the

Geese flying North in September?

Alright, soldier boy.

You can't tell the worth of a man

By the color of his collar.

SENSES

Does propaganda imitate life

Or does life imitate propaganda?

What about another option? Or a few?

Sight is truth but eyes deceive.

We can't even believe everything we read.

Smell triggers memories,

Some say the truest sense,

But it is not easy to reflect your ideas

With scents.

If newspapers were scratch and sniff

I bet the headlines would focus their attentions

Elsewhere.

If I relate a story or anecdote

About what I heard,

Someone might tell me I heard wrong.

Now, what if I heard clearly and precisely

What was said?

Would I have heard wrong?

Or merely been subjected to

A removed morsel of information,

Nonetheless, heard it correctly.

Just a taste,

A bad taste in your mouth,

Tastefully done,

There is no accounting for taste to some.

But if something touches you,

Do you complain about your personal space?

A touch,

Just a touch,

A touching moment…

All these questions,

Some might say I'm a bit touched in the head.

109

SPAGHETTI LEFT TO BOIL IN THE PASTA POT

The remnants dance in the water boiling,

Performing, angelic sea anemones, a ghostly shade,

Dancing freely, moving to currents

As if they were sound.

But what I perceive as performance

May be what will bring about the demise of the dance,

And the ballet that has inspired me

May be the torture to end

Of this animate.

But for choice or force,

I'm not sure which,

The dance will continue

Till end.

110

SEMANTICS

The world can be broken down, disassembled,

By semantics.

Words are words,

They can be cultivated or wielded by powerful people

Or people who harness power in some form.

But when all is basic,

People are the controllers, the channels,

The good and the bad.

I have been part of over enamored debates

Forgetting about opinion and perception,

Wildly staking my point,

But beyond the words was feeling, intention.

The words were merely a path,

Though in some cases a stubborn one,

Towards a destination,

Perhaps a new point of vantage.

Alas and with joy,

Words are one of the mainstays of communication

But how often does an averted glance,

Or a hint of a smile

Belie the words said, and instead

Convey the meanings behind the curtain of words.

Words are useful

But are nothing absent of intent.

And the placation of ones vocabulary and knowledge

By way of immense verbalization on subjects mundane or

arbitrary

Tends to lose my interest quickly…

Further helping me to understand

Why eyes sometimes glaze as

I go on about things of which I know.

Sad it is to ignore those conversations altogether,

For possibility of missing something interesting,

Or possibly educational, enlightening.

Words can be paint

But their flow, their passion,

Their meaning is up to their orator's intent

And are subject to the minds, ears and lives

Of those receiving these transmissions

Of idea,

Perception,

And feeling.

THOUGHTS OF WESTERN TINSEL

The sky is falling!

At least it's a beautiful sunset.

The sky is falling

And yes,

We will be closer to the stars.

But then,

We will always have the moon.

PLACES UNDER STREETLIGHTS

Places are just footsteps,

And the places that I've been

Might be enough in lesson

To question the contents

Within your chest,

A hollow cavity with unrest the decay,

Though flourishing as malcontent,

I join indignant fray.

A battle I could win,

A war could wear me out.

Life seems merely strategic assumptions

Projected onto clout.

But only if a mouth would not speak up.

No lack of saying, but

Words that come to light,

A savior with something to say,

To help make a street bright.

113

TO PRETEND LOVE IS HANDCUFFS

Who shoots down the idealist?

A face so flawed but beautiful,

An altruist who just lives,

The eyes of hope not dimming.

A single drop of water on the beach goes unnoticed

But when the tide comes in, the beach steps back.

This foot after foot and again, motivation,

Not invasion,

Passive integration

But with action,

It carves a path through the static,

Those refusing to move or be moved.

To pretend love is handcuffs,

Distracted muse,

A heart could break with every breath

And every kiss.

114.

PRESERVATIVES

And maybe that's the reason

They fill us full of preservatives,

To keep us

From going bad.

115

THE WALLS, THE BARS

Just Like that

Perception can change.

Where once you saw contempt,

Perhaps your own reflection,

Now you see the overlooked

Generosity

For no reason

Perhaps,

Other than familiarity.

Thank you.

Still there are some things,

Some needles of disdain,

But those sting much less now.

Maybe they are just a

Misinterpretation that

Until now

You figured was true,

And if the patronizing remarks

Are intended,

Then they can be laughed about,

They don't hurt anymore.

The walls, the bars you feel hold you inside,

They are yours to be held by

Or they are yours to deny,

You are free.

116

RIGORS OF A ROAD TRIP

Senseless talking,

So many unnecessary injuries,

Words cut just to hear them.

The bridges sing and the towns blur,

Conversation is sporadic and painful.

Some towns built with a king in mind

And pink hotels and rainbow colored factories,

All different landscapes in a same ol' same ol'.

Impressions are fuzzy lines

Blurred to attenuate reality,

Or to show the beauty beneath

What is taken for granted.

You can gauge the miles

By the change in the trees.

Some places look like home,

Some places feel like home,

And some places you just don't get a feeling for.

Despondent feelings,

They can fade quickly when you are with good friends,

Long as you aren't taking them for granted.

Our cars are conveniences we see as our right

But when they work fine,

Do we consider ourselves lucky?

While thinking of the roads and country

Of our previous travels,

Do we appreciate the way to our next endeavor,

To our next domicile?

It is easy to see the day's light fading,

But to notice the sun filtering through the trees

Painting lovely golden leaves,

Do we realize the view?

A blessing to see! Truly,

I'm happy to be.

117

FOSSILS, FUEL OR SOMETHING ELSE?

Grinds and Numbers

Is what we are seeing,

Grids and numbers

Is what we are being.

Truth be told,

We live in a lie.

It's not our selves,

But the life we buy.

Outlines of chalk

Are parking spots

For them who want,

Yet muster as have naughts,

While the wind blows the paper around the ether

Pushing us back and forth as we are neither.

All the gas is free if it's on T.V.

Break your hump to pay at the pump,

Consumed as you consump.

Believing what we read, screaming

"Don't Tread On Me!"

118

SUNRISE AND JETLAG

Sky was a bruised horizon

Making way to a ruby mist

Set on an undefined slab.

Now a spectrum, full color

Reaches from earth to sky.

All colors, all colors.

Civilizations are circuits below,

I pass them by towards a sight of pure beauty,

A new day.

Planting foot to earth during the ascent,

Not to overshoot

But to begin.

Beginning, though I started

At least in motion, at least in thought,

Now to start moving, people, minds, hearts,

Self.

New to me, in doing.

Ah the sunrise.

Such colors and timbres of light

Exist only in real life.

My eloquence not precise enough to describe,

If even words could do justice,

This awesome vision.

A gift to me,

To all those who wish to see,

I'm thankful.

A mountain is a kitten,

You could touch the relief from up here.

Does anyone else see this?

The ruby curtain falls to reveal,

A vast expanse of possibility.

Sunrise.

FLYING BACK EAST

I think the security guards

At the airport

Stole my gum.

I didn't realize peppermint

Was a security risk.

Flight is leaving

About 40 minutes late.

It's strange being on a plane.

THE ARTIST'S HAND

Staring at a black and white drawing,

I could only see it as an abstract.

But as perception adjusted

And then I saw the artist's hand,

I noticed how strange indeed it is,

To be enamored with the undefined,

Yet, despondent towards the recognized.

In the same moment I realized

How completely not strange that is.

WHAT IS HOME?

The scent, lavender.

The color is lavender.

What makes a house, home?

SAVING HOPE IN AN EMPTY BOTTLE

Every bottle you break

Is some hope that's erased,

And I don't want to be

The master of your misery.

ASHES LEFT BEHIND

I offer you an olive branch with a trembling hand

You set it afire with the cinders in your eyes.

Now smoke is pouring from the offer of peace I made to

you

As your ego ignites a fire of anger in me.

Oh please, help me keep my cool

And not be consumed by the blaze been set

By you and me, to feel this heat it's just not worth it.

In my mind I see your end through an angry haze

Your demise a thousand times in an instant.

But in truth my heart wishes not for you to come to harm,

Only that you could see yourself the way I do.

I have cut another olive branch

And I hold it close to my chest

Because I have made peace within myself

And now I see you as nothing but the ashes left

Behind.

124

LOOKING BACK IS JUST LAUGHS AND TEARS

The Sun slinks slow across a Winter sky

The afternoon yawns as the evening rubs its eyes

Yesterday's anguish on the ground covered in flies

The carrion of broken hearts, burned bridges and severed ties.

The pity on a heart that's done being broke

Melts away like laughter after the punch line of a joke

Strike a match to old love letters, watch them all go up in smoke

How could the word seem foreign now when aloud it's spoke?

And all the time

Does not belong to you or I

After it's gone we say, "my how it flies"

But still we try

To hide our footsteps from our own eyes

To ourselves we tell the biggest lies

But why turn away from truth

Or honesty despise?

What's the point of holding on

To the things you're glad when they are gone?

After you know that you've moved on

What's the point of holding on?

Memories and places in time

All have a purpose

All valid in our minds

Some we see as heroic deeds

Some we see as crimes,

Victories and losses

Are all just points upon a line

But love that's ever been true,

Love that's ever been felt for real

Is nothing to be denied

Because guilt won't let you heal,

And there's no point in holding on

To the things you're glad when they are gone

Forever you'll remember but move on

Because there's no point in holding on

To what's gone.

125

CARPENTER WASTE

I'd be carpenter waste

If my Dad didn't see it through.

It doesn't mean the same to me

As it does to you.

And for all the glory one could prove,

It's much more than I care to lose.

Remember snow melting on tin roof?

A rhythm pounding so profuse,

Amidst thoughts of death and youth,

It reminds me, it's more than nail and tooth.

I'm not scared to say I care

And if the Reaper's knife

Does take my life,

Well, I'll be found on the ground,

Where the flowers grow proud all around.

126.

THROUGH THE FOREST OF A DOUBTFUL MIND

The water fell from the sky

And grew a thorn right in my side.

Getting fat on humble pie,

The fates conspired

To their desires

Stockpiling tinder

For their pyres.

I saw the thorn

And felt its tear,

Slow and sharp enough

To numb it's wake.

I felt its presence on the air

And prayed my Lord,

My soul to take.

127

PLAYING FOR THE KING

The Jester is rewarded for entertaining,

Executed for annoying or challenging.

Challenges the King right under his regal nose

At risk of discovering a hanging.

Juggles moods,

Jokes with sincerity,

Contorts the body so the face may change.

Plays at magic, cards close to vest,

Plays their win

Does not contest.

CRESCENT CITY, CA

Feet, wet.

Jacket, wet.

Hat, wet.

Wet.

Everything is wet.

Rain falling dutifully since we got,

Automotively speaking,

Shanghaied in this town

Two or three days ago.

At this point, it could have been 100 days ago.

Our ups constantly losing ground

In their battle with our downs,

And manic situations provide enough fuel

For rapid mood swings.

This small town,

They call it a city,

Is a nice place and reminds me

Occasionally of home,

Despite the nearly constant rainfall

And temperatures in the upper 50's during January.

A nice place to breakdown

But I wouldn't want to breakdown there.

Perhaps we are lucky

To have the fuel pump on the van go.

Which, in a bittersweet kind of medicine,

We also find the U-joint needs to be replaced too,

Before severe damage occurs from not addressing the

situation.

And what do ya' know,

It isn't that expensive to fix it.

Okay, go ahead.

Everything is still wet as we wait

For the mechanic to finish the repairs.

At least we got a chance to briefly

Experience the Pacific for the first time in our lives.

Soaking wet and still searching for water.

The irony is heavy with humor.

He plays bass, the mechanic tells us,

And didn't like Country Music until

It was infused into the Rock world

During the 70's.

He's a nice guy with a wife and twins, our mechanic.

I'm almost always skeptical about mechanics.

At least, the ones I don't know.

129.

WORDS ARE THROWN

Hurled to the side,

Girl derived turmoil spoiled a friendship

Almost entirely.

Neither one wanted to see the face,

Let alone the side,

Or be in the same place at the same time.

Injured pride hardest to heal,

Hard for the record to be sealed,

Transgressions from both while emotions reeled

From an unintended attack, causing anger forth and back.

Guts were spilt over feelings of guilt,

Something so huge seemed to make the world tilt.

Stubborn and self-righteous,

Neither one liked this.

But none gave up much ground,

Just built up walls around themselves,

Put years of friendship on respective bookshelves.

They say time heals all wounds

But apparently leaves scars,

A two hour trip with no words

While riding in the same car.

Never was there injury intent

But when discovered,

Apologies were said and meant,

But mistrust hovered.

Some people wondered if they'd ever recover

From a misunderstanding and a dishonest lover.

Time has moved on and those friends are still together

Dealing with their own storms, and handling the same

weather.

It's good to see that their ties were not severed,

My question is now,

Is their friendship worse,

Or has it gotten better?

130.

AT THE GALLERY

All the canvas painted and pasted,

Faces, blank staring and wasted,

And me among them.

Staring, trying to look

And shook, by the art but not it's intent.

Just staring and feeling my feeling spent

Wondering where the money went.

Not caring, no emotions flaring, just staring.

Facsimiles of bursts,

Sure, we all thirst,

So apparent, as dry lips are pursed.

And no one wants the pin, no one wants to sin

Against the fold, but after the first,

What is the point to be rehearsed? The want is win

Not taking chances being bold.

But peacock words make pictures live,

Like the point of a jailhouse shiv.

Drawing upon the inspiration of victims

Not knowing, their crimson makes the scene.

In times of lean like this, the fat is chewed,

And replicas on the landscape tattooed

Like memories forgotten, none held beholden.

The wind moves too fast to allow anyone to grasp

A tether to the balloon aloft in weather,

Not hot, not wet, as honorable as brigands bets.

Only making words for the point of comment and

commerce

With eyes affixed not on subject, but towards a hazy, vague

purse.

And cordial nods rehearsed for contact, face first,

As the backs soon turn and those bubbles of praise are

burst.

Through the glass all stained

By the spittle of charlatans with rhetoric unchained,

Some rays of light and hope

Make the altars, unscathed by the glut and the gloat,

Luminous, making an ark from a boat.

In this house they're the edges un-planed

The felt, the solid, amidst darkness a welcomed grope.

The muse for the lyric that will float, unfettered,

From inspired throats.

131

SILVER GELATIN ANALYSIS OF DARK EYES

The children look forward into

The mysterious eye that stares back,

Cold, black, indifferent.

Life for them is as simple as it

Has ever been at that age.

It was harder back then, they say,

But family photographs belie

Head above water,

Security for Mother, Son and Daughter.

Secure in the model cast upon,

But eyes are where the truth hides.

Proud provider with façade,

Background shroud,

House built by stone

But out of clouds.

Of himself and the family *he* built

His head is swollen.

The posture of his lovely wife,

Reserved and proper,

As she gazes 1,000 miles

With eyes demure and crestfallen.

Girlhood memories of summer fields

Filled with wildflowers,

And the notions of the true love

She would one day marry.

All well and all good

To imagine during childhood,

Of lovely holidays in *their* palace

On a hill somewhere,

Till her world confines

As are drawn the lines

Of the box in which

She must now exist,

Giving care to *a* husband

And *her* children,

While far away she still sees those days

When her life was her own

And expectations seemed like destiny.

132

SOMETIMES YOUR CLOSEST FRIENDS...

Pardon me friend,

But those were exactly

Where they were supposed to

Be.

What gives you the right to say

Where they go?

Then again, what gives me the right

To tell you where anything goes,

Or even tell *anything*

Where *it* goes.

Enough of this bickering,

The scenery sometimes was

Spoiled by lingering insults,

And none are to blame and

All are to be blamed.

Enough of this dysfunction

We need production, no more distraction

It's time for us to do.

Pardon me my friend.

I'm sorry.

133.

IF NEARLY UNEXPLAINABLE

With her words

She spoke to me,

With her voice she spoke

To all.

Like sledgehammers

One after one,

Pounding me with

Subtle messages so relevant

And I wonder

Can she read my mind?

Yet her words, her inferring

So obtusely casual

Like wisps of familiar

Earthy fragrances that

Blatantly suggest life as

Winter bows out to Spring.

Called in simile

"A cleansing experience",

Words from a friend reflect

My own perception yet,

Something so different,

Personal,

Nearly, if maybe

Unexplainable.

She helped me realize

My own to be ridiculous

To the point where I felt

Sorry for her in her insecurity,

She need not be insecure.

134

WORKING POOR ARTIST

Slouching shoulder, strong of back,

At least enough to be

Of unnoticed use, unnoticed use.

When it's gone you cry though,

Cry as if entitled, cry as if entitled.

Suckle on expectations,

A milk of fear, a milk of doubt.

The gnashing teeth of maturity

Tear at dreams,

And all is all of nothing

But presence, but intent, but actions.

Measures are what we see,

A graduated self,

A scale to say another way,

What we want we should give.

All say all should go free,

But freedom feels of knife in back

Or spit in face.

So sorry from the past

When that is all you see,

But memories are fond.

When you hear, see or read the art,

You feel a, "why the anger?"

Then you think

And say, "oh", I understand.

I understand what?

Merely that I have felt.

Good

But there is more than the anger felt.

The joy shines through.

135

BABY ON THE DOORSTEP

The baby on the doorstep is fully clothed

The baby on the doorstep fully knows

The baby on the doorstep is only trying to pull the wool

Over my eyes again.

The baby on the doorstep wants to come in

The baby on the doorstep calls me friend

I call him the same but I've got to wonder,

Oh yes I wonder.

You are not a baby

You are a grown man

You are driving me crazy

And I know you understand.

The baby on the doorstep wants my help

The baby on the doorstep says he's not well

The baby on the doorstep wants me to be his father

But he doesn't bother writing home.

The baby on the doorstep wants to come in

The baby on the doorstep calls me friend

I call him the same but I've got to wonder,

Oh yes I wonder

Whose child he is.

136

THE OLD MAN AND THE SEA

The day's first light

Not yet shown,

The Old Man rises from his slumber.

With a creaking back

And an ancient groan,

His years have his body humbled.

But though body may be tired,

Mind is willing.

His lifelong passion afire,

His life's purpose fulfilling

And as the waves rush the shore,

He's younger than ever before.

A truer romance has never had he,

This Old Fisherman and the Sea.

The Sunrise greets him

As he steps out the door,

His vessel is ready

He shoves off from the shore,

The land grows distant behind him

He looks out upon the Sea,

And the azure reminds him

There's no place he'd rather be.

And the waves rush the shore,

He's as young as ever before,

A truer romance has never had he,

This Fisherman and his Sea.

137

WHY IS GOD FEARED MORE

OFTEN THAN LOVED?

Why is God feared more often than loved?

Regardless of "belief",

Even atheists, even Christians,

All faiths seem to have faith

In the Almighty smite-ings,

Blame hurled at a deity,

But rarely thanks or love

Consented even, towards

"the Creator"?

Taken for granted such things

As the picturesque sunrise or sunset,

The intricate systems

Endocrine, digestive, respiratory, circulatory,

Habitats, ecologies, geographies.

Our mind itself

And its abilities to think free,

Free enough to destroy our own selves,

Or our owned selves.

Free enough to be inspired

And to format that unutterable, yet

Through leagues, legions, lands,

Loud resounding feeling into a mural,

A brushstroke,

A soliloquy, a whisper,

And to not see, that

Other than our words,

Which hardly ever satisfy the thought

Much less the feeling,

Other than our pictures,

Other than our music,

Musings and passion,

Sorrows, defeats, successes,

The shiver of new love

Laying hand on naked belly,

Other than a tear

Brought out of tough façade

To stroll poignantly down cheek

From recognition, finally,

Of something truly beautiful,

That there is more which resonates in us,

Around us, from us and without us.

To see these, even feel them and ask,

"Where is God?"

Is to miss the point.

God is dead God is alive God is element God is.

No matter what name,

No matter what face,

And those who try to own God,

Merely own fear.

And maybe,

That is why God is feared more often than loved.

138

FOR A FRIEND IN GRIEVING

A passing glance seems

All we have

On the precipice of end

Though no truer treasure

Can we claim

Than to know we were dear friends

Some may come into our lives

And leave with no footprint

Before the snow

Some will last through

Winters indefinite

And help us to find Spring's first show

These we can say are

The true ones we have

With us through laughter, tears and fuss

And in their honor

We must remember too

That through all seasons they also have us.

139

INNER, OUTER, BEYOND

My words, my actions,

They are the atmosphere of who I am.

To say in that context,

I am a man.

A person to be seen and dealt with,

Tolerated and desired in presence.

Of the next, to know my heart,

To ask of my intent,

These are all rockets which push

Through the sky.

But if outside eyes

Look only to set upon the Moon,

Not to embrace the matter

Seen only as nothingness,

Where does exist the unspoken of all?

Were there a painter aboard

They would use black and white to establish

Plane and figure

Denying neither in motion

Towards that state,

That state of seeing and being nothing,

Yet all as the observer.

Were there not eyes to see,

And hearts and minds to be

Touched,

All this would exist

As we suppose and accept

But only in our context.

Without eyes

Or hearts and minds,

All matter may be in place.

But as all darkness and points of light,

Without reference

How would we understand?

How important would that be

If there was no we?

In reference to me,

As a point of light or

Part of the darkness,

My existence is the

Greatness of eternity

And the minutiae of vision.

140.

A TOAST

I toast you

As my drink spills

Through a hole in the

Bottom of my cup.

And now I question,

Continue with the toast?

Or imbibe quickly

While the drink fills the glass?

What place for honor

Next to self preservation,

The former is gone when

The latter is all of

Your concern.

141

WIND, WATER, PATIENCE

I am shaping as I am shaped,

What I do unto others

I do also unto myself,

As their acts affect they and I

In one breath.

What force does change the hard, hard stone?

The stand fast, ancient mountain,

The sharp peaks of earlier times

Now round and modest,

And why?

What force could conduct the form

Of such reticent fortitude?

As simple as the softness of the wind

And the water which went against it,

Bending to carve through it,

And through patient persistence,

To move it.

142

I AM HERE

I spend a lot of time thinking about yesterday

It's a comfortable place to visit, but it is impossible to stay

As the hands go around and now becomes then

And the place where I am becomes a place where I've been

Becoming fond in the favor of when, a simple game I often play

Pulling the black and the white into their own, independent of the grey

And there they lay, in present's envy I yearn their magic once again

But there is no way, past's magic to the future can only wisdom lend.

Yet the future lays always an inch past my grasp

Reaching through now 'til around it's splendor my hands clasp

Alas, a carrot as food for thought, not meant for a meal

Scrambling over myself and the moment, errant cast of rod and reel

Perchance to steal an instant of what I want from what

might be

Then, a glance at my empty hands on a good day get's a

laugh from me

Past my hands and looking down, the ground I see and all

of here and now

To be present and in time to feel my own life, to understand

real

And to find my how.